The Book of the Angel

Table of Contents

Chapter 1..4
Chapter 2..6
Chapter 3..8
Chapter 4..10
Chapter 5..12
Chapter 6..14
Chapter 7..16
Chapter 8..18
Chapter 9..20
Chapter 10..22
Chapter 11..24
Chapter 12..26
Chapter 13..28
Chapter 14..30
Chapter 15..32
Chapter 16..34
Chapter 17..36
Chapter 18..38
Chapter 19..40
Chapter 20..42
Chapter 21..44

Book 11 "The Sermon of the Angel"

Chapter 1
Sunday - First Reading

When John in his Gospel speaks of the Word, that is he who is, and has ever been, with the Father and the Holy Ghost, one God, In this one God, there are truly Three Persons; yet not three Gods, for in the Three Persons is only one divinity, the one, perfect Godhead, belonging equally to each; and in the Three Persons, only one will, one wisdom, one power, one beauty, one strength, one love, one joy.

The Word, then, being for ever one with the Father and the Holy Ghost, is truly God. A familiar word like ONE can help us, perhaps, to understand - for each of the three letters is necessary to the whole, and we cannot take away one letter without destroying the meaning. So in God, there must ever be the Three Persons, equal in all things, with all things equally in each, for there can be no dividing of God. There was no dividing when the Word, the Son of God, took a human nature; he was not separated, by this, from the Father and the Holy Ghost. He took our human nature, yet remained ever the Word of God. His human nature was necessary for him, to achieve our salvation. It can help us to understand this if we consider how our thoughts and our words are not things we can see or touch, except in so far as writing gives them a more material existence.

The Word of God, the Son of God, could not have come as one of us, or lived with us, for our salvation, unless he had taken on our human nature. A written word can be seen and read, then understood, then spoken. The Son of God can be seen, in that flesh he took to himself, and so we can understand and have no doubt that he is one with the Father and the Holy Ghost. Truly then, there are Three Persons, undivided, unchanging and unchangeable, eternally in all things equal, Three, yet but one God. Since God is eternal and timeless, all things were eternally known to him, before their existence in time.

Then, when he willed them to be, they came to be with that exact perfection which suited their purpose. The divine wisdom of God willed all things to be what they are for his own honour and glory. He had no need of them; it was not to make up for any deficiency in himself - something wanting to his goodness or joy - there can be no defect or deficiency in God. It was his love, and his love alone, which led him to create; that there might be beings, apart from himself, whose existence should be an existence of joy, deriving from his own being an joy. All things, then, foreseen by God, and present to him eternally, though as yet uncreated, had already that design and perfection which they would possess when his creating brought them to be.

One thing excelled all others, designed and perfected by God with a special joy. This was Mary, the Virgin who was a Mother, the Mother who was ever a Virgin.

It has been said that all created things are made up of four elements - fire, air, water and earth. If so, then in Mary's pure body, these elements were to have a special perfection: the air should be fittingly an image of the Holy Ghost; the earth should be rich and fruitful, for the growth of useful things, to supply every need; the water should be calm and unmenacing, unruffled by every wind; and the fire so strong and bright that all the earth should be warmed by it, and the heavens themselves.

Virgin Mary, we know that in you the design and perfection willed by God have come to be. As he foresaw you, so he has perfectly created you. And of all his creation, you most please him. The Father rejoiced that he would do so much through you: the Son rejoiced in your holiness and love: the Holy Ghost rejoiced in your lowliness and obedience. The Father's joy is that of the Son and the Holy Ghost: the Son's joy is that of the Father and Spirit: and the Holy Ghost's joy is that of the Father and the Son.

Father, Son and Holy Ghost rejoice in you, the one joy of Three who are One. Father, Son and Holy Ghost love you, Mary, the love of the Three Persons, One God.

Chapter 2
Sunday - Second Reading

Mary, we know that you were ever in the mind of God, before his creating brought you to be - the most perfect of all his creatures. He knew you as Noe, before the flood, knew the Ark he was to build, and the way he was to build it. The design of the Ark had been made known to him, and he waited for the time when God would command him to set to work. The design and perfection, Mary, of your glorious body, the Ark of God, was known to God before all time. And he knew the time when he would bring it into being by his creating. As Noe rejoiced at the thought of the Ark he was to build, so God rejoiced, Mary, at the thought of you. Noe's Ark would withstand the storms; you, Mary, the Ark of God, would withstand, in the strength of your holiness, every attack of the hatred and sin of hell.

Noah's Ark was so built that no water could seep in - a ship whose timbers were carefully protected both inside and out. You, Mary, the Ark of God, would be so strong in God's grace, anointed and protected by his Holy Ghost, that no desire would ever enter your heart, either for your own glory or for the possession of earthly things. Such desires, we know, are as displeasing to God as the water which seeps into the keel of a ship, and collecting there becomes state and offensive.

Noe was pleased at the size and capacity of his Ark. God rejoiced, Mary, in that holiness which would be yours, in your love which would embrace all creatures, and in your gentleness which would look with pity on sinners, and hate only what was hateful to him. But most of all, he rejoiced in that ever increasing grace which would fit you to bear in your womb that which heaven and earth could not contain, the Person of God the Son, to hold him and be truly his Mother.

Noe took pride, as every captain of a ship takes pride, in the cleanliness and tidiness and brightness of the Ark. God rejoiced, Mary, in your virginity, for in you there would be no sin, nor slightest stain of sin, to taint your perfection. Noe provided for himself and those with him, all that was needed to survive the days ahead. God chose you, Mary, for his Son, that your body should provide for him a perfect human body. Noe came from the Ark unchanged. But from you, Mary, the Ark of God, the Son of God came forth, clothed with that pure flesh and blood which he had taken from you.

When Noe left the Ark, its purpose was served - it was empty and useless. But when Christ came forth from your womb, you were filled with every gift of the Holy Ghost, growing ever in holiness, not further now from Christ, but nearer to him, and dearer even than before, united to him on earth and in heaven for ever.

Chapter 3
Sunday - Third Reading

From the moment of God's promise, through the long years of waiting, Abraham loved the son who was to be his, the child who would be called Isaac. How much more did God love you, Virgin Mary, whom he had foreseen from eternity, and knew before your creating, for he knew also the joy your birth would be to him. Abraham did not know how his love for God would be tested and proved through his promised son.

But God knew with his divine knowledge how through you, Mary, his great love for man would be made known. Abraham knew that Isaac would be born of his union with Sarah, a child conceived unexpectedly in their old age. God knew that his Son would be conceived in you, Virgin Mary, without the intervention of man, and be born of you, true Mother yet ever a Virgin. Abraham knew that his son once conceived would grow without his help to become a person, independent of his father. God knew that the sacred body of his Son, formed in your womb, would in a special way, be for ever most intimately united with the Godhead. This must be so, since the Son is ever in the Father, the Father in the Son, equal yet one.

Abraham knew that he and his son must return to dust in the corruption of death. God would not allow your pure body, Mary, to see corruption, for it was the flesh and blood of your body which had been given to form the body of his Son. Abraham built a house for the son who was to be born to him. But God himself, the Blessed Trinity, is the dwelling in which you, Mary, will abide for ever. In a wonderful way, then, your dwelling, Mary, was in God, who surrounded you with his protecting love. Yet God dwelt ever in you, leading you to the highest holiness by his presence. For his promised son, Abraham prepared wheat, wine and oil, three kinds of essential nourishment.

For you, Virgin Mary, God himself was to be your eternal meal, Father, Son and Holy Ghost, Three yet One. And through you he was to give himself to men as the food of life. So we may attribute this food of life in a way, to you, Mary, since it is by you that it has come to us. The three things which Abraham prepared can be thought of as a sign of the action of the Three Persons. Oil cannot burn without a wick. This can suggest to us That the love of God the Father could not be made known on earth without the humanity of the Son, that humanity which he took from you, his Virgin Mother.

Wheat was to be made into flour, and then bread, for our daily use. The Son of God, though he is truly the food of Angels, could not be our food without that flesh and blood which he took from your loving womb. Wine cannot refresh us unless it is in something we can drink from. The Holy Ghost could not be poured out upon us without the humanity of your Son. For the salvation which Christ's Passion and Death accomplished is the fount of all the delights and graces bestowed by God on Angels and on men.

Chapter 4
Monday - First Reading

It was love that led God to create. There could be nothing lacking in God, nothing wanting to his goodness or his joy.

It was out of love alone that he willed creation, that there might be beings, apart from himself, who would partake of his infinite goodness and joy. So the Angels came to be, created by God in countless numbers. To them he gave free will, freedom to act, in accordance with their nature, as they willed. As he himself is under no necessity but has created out of love alone, he will that the Angels, whom he designed for eternal happiness with him, should likewise be under no necessity.

He looked for love in response to his love, obedience to his offer of eternal joy.

Yet in the first moment of their creation, there were Angels who chose, freely and deliberately against their Creator, in spite of his infinite love, which called them to love in return. Justly they fell, fixed in their evil will, from an eternal joy into an eternal misery. But not all fell. To those Angels who chose love for love, there was given the contemplation of God in all his glory, power and holiness. From this contemplation, they came to know the eternity of God, that he has no beginning and no end; they learnt what it meant to have him for their Creator; and they saw most clearly how everything they possessed had come to them from his love and his power.

They learnt too that his wisdom had given them a wisdom of their own, bu which he allowed them to foresee the future. And it was a joy and consolation to them to know that God in his mercy and love wished to replace, in his own way, those Angels who had forfeited by pride and envy their place in heaven.

In their contemplation of God, the Angels saw with wonder a throne placed next to that of God himself. They knew that the one for whom this throne had been prepared had not yet been created. Yet already they loved this chosen one, and rejoiced as they waited. Their love for each other was born of their love for God. But between these two loves they saw one who was more lovable than themselves, one whom God loves with great joy more than all his creatures. Virgin Mary, you were the chosen one, destined for that throne near to the throne of God.

It was you whom the Angels loved, after God, from the first moment of their creation, seeing in the contemplation of God, how beautiful he had made themselves, but how much more beautiful he would make you. They saw that in you there would be a love and a joy far greater than their own. They saw too the crown that awaited you, a crown of glory and beauty surpassed only by the majesty of God. They knew how God their Creator was glorified by themselves and they rejoiced. They knew how much more he would be glorified by you, and they rejoiced still more.

Before ever you were created, Mary, God and Angels together rejoiced in you.

Chapter 5
Monday - Second Reading

God's creation of the world and all it contains took place in the instant of his will's expression; and with that design and perfection foreseen by him. Yet there remained still uncreated another work of creation which would surpass what he had already done. You, Mary, are, as it were, another world, a world which God foresaw with greater joy, a world the Angels were more pleased to contemplate, a world of more benefit to those of good will that the whole earth and all it contains.

Mary, we may see in God's act of creation and in all created things an image of your creating. We read that it pleased God to separate the darkness from the light when he created the earth. How much more it pleased him to enlighten you from childhood. The darkness, the time of your infancy, was made light by your knowledge of God, your understanding of God, and the will to love for God which day by day led you on to a love surpassed only by the love of God.

The mental darkness of childhood, without knowledge of God, without reasoning power to guide, is for us a time of defencelessness and danger. But we know that for you, exempt from sin, it was a time of purest innocence. We read that it pleased God to make, together with the stars, two lights - the sun for daytime, the moon for the night. It pleased God still more, Mary, to set in you two heavenly lights, brighter and more beautiful than the sun or the moon: the first - perfect obedience, a radiant light for Angels and men to admire, guiding all who saw it to God himself, who is the light of eternal day; the second - a most complete and trusting faith, the light to men in the darkness of despair and unbelief when your Son chose suffering and death, a light to cast out all shadow of doubt and uncertainty when he rose from the dead. We read that it pleased God to create the stars. The thoughts of your heart, Mary, were more pleasing to him.

We read that it pleased God to create the birds, whose flight and song are a delight to men. All the words which you spoke, Mary, heard also in heaven to the joy of the Angels, were more pleasing still. We read that God created the earth itself, the dry land and the soul; and flowering and fruit-bearing trees of many kinds. Your life, Mary, your occupations and work, were more pleasing to him, for you would give nourishment, and life itself, to all, and your love would make each act of your life more beautiful to God and the Angels than the fairest of flowers are to men. God created the plants, flowers, trees, and fruits, minerals, metals, and precious stones - he has made the earth rich with these things.

Yet he saw in you, Mary, even before your creating, more qualities and virtues than in all earthly things. We read that God's creation was pleasing to him, and that he looked with joy on all he had done. It pleased him still more to create you, Mary, and he looked with greater joy on you, even before your creating, than on this earth and all earthly things. That world and everything in it, - all would be destroyed. Though created before you, Mary, it would not endure. But you, by God's eternal decree, were created to be for ever, and to be for ever united to him in deepest love, created in fullest grace, responding to his grace in all things, and so growing to the perfection of holiness.

Chapter 6
Monday - Third Reading

God is the Creator of all beings, and he is Being itself. Nothing can be or come to be without God. Therefore, this world and all things in it owe their existence to him alone. He is the Creator of all. And Creator, last of all, of Man. To mankind he gave, as he had given to the Angels, the gift of free will. He wished that be free choice man would cling to what was good, and so avoid a just punishment and earn a just reward. Among men, little regard is paid to work done unwillingly, under threat of punishment.

We honour work done willingly out of love, and it is such work that deserves reward. It pleased God rather to leave them free, making known what a reward obedience would win, and what punishment pride and disobedience would incur. God created man, forming him from the dust of the earth. He looked for man's love and obedient service, that so the the places of those Angels who had disobeyed in their pride, and fallen from joy into misery, might be filled once more. They should have received a crown of joy for their love and obedience. Instead, they lost their reward, hating not only the joy they had forfeited but also those virtues which would have assured it to them.

A king is given a crown of gold, calling all to honour him who wears it. But there is a heavenly crown for each virtue, calling even to men on earth to honour one who loves God, calling to Angels in heaven to rejoice, calling to God to reward. What of the crown of God himself? In him all virtues reside, surpassing in every way every other possible good. In him all is virtue. Yet three special virtues stand out in what we know of God, three crowns of incomparable glory. First, that he created the Angels. (It was the envy of such glory that led some of them into their pride and fall.) Second, that he created Man. (The loss of God's glory was man's most grievous loss, when in his folly he let himself be led into sin.) Third, that he created you, Virgin Mary.

The fall of Angels and of man did not lessen the virtue of God, or take from his crown of glory. They were created for God's honour, and they refused it, it is true, just as they were created for their own desire, and yet forfeited it by sin. The wisdom of God turned their sin into an even greater glory for himself. For your creation, Mary, gave such glory to God, that what was refused him by Angels and men was made good a thousand times over. Virgin Mary, our Queen and our hope of salvation, you may truly be called the crown of God's honour. Through you he showed his divine virtue.

From you he won honour and glory greater than from all other creatures. The Angels knew, even before your creating, that by your holiness and humility you would overcome the pride of the Devil and his hatred for man. They had seen how man had fallen into misery, but in their contemplation of God, they still rejoiced, knowing well what great things God would do, Mary, through your lowliness, when his creating brought you to be.

Chapter 7
Tuesday - First Reading

We read in the Bible of Adam's original state of happiness. Then of his disobedience to God, which brought so much suffering and sorrow. We are not told that he continued in disobedience. From his conduct after Cain had killed Abel, his refraining from intercourse with Eve until he knew that this was no longer the will of God, we may judge that the love and service of God was his first thought. His sorrow was not so much the unhappiness he had brought on himself, but rather the offence he had committed against God.

Created by God, owing his existence and his happiness to God, he had turned against God, and so justly deserved God's anger. This was true sorrow, bringing with it repentance and humility. And with this true sorrow came also consolation from God. One thing, and one thing only, could have fully consoled him - the promise that God himself should come as man, of Adam's own race, and by love and humility redeem that race which his pride had deprived of life.

That God should be born as men are born was unthinkable. Adam and Eve owed their beginning in some way to a special creation by God. Even this would not be fitting for the coming of God to earth. It would seem that Adam understood from God's words something of what was to be. At least, we may picture him foreseeing the future, foreseeing a woman, like Eve in womanhood, but lovelier and holier than all of his race, a virgin and mother, bringing God himself to this world. We may think of him grieving at the words spoken to Eve by the Devil.

But rejoicing, his sorrow turned to joy, at the thought, Mary, of your words to the Angel. We may think of him grieving that Eve his wife, created by God from his body, had deceived him and drawn him on to eternal death. But rejoicing that you, Virgin Mary, would bear in all purity Christ, the Son of God, to restore man to life. Grieving that Eve's first act was of disobedience; rejoicing that you, Mary, would be a daughter of God, most dear to him in all things, ever obedient to his will.

Grieving that Eve had been tempted, in the sight of God and all the Angels, by the false promise of being made like to God; rejoicing that in the sight of God and the Angels, you, Mary, would acknowledge yourself the Handmaid of God. Grieving that Eve had offended God, and brought about the condemnation of man; rejoicing that your word to God should bring such joy to yourself and to all men. Grieving that Eve had closed to man the gate of heaven; rejoicing that your word had opened that gate again to yourself and to all who sought to enter. So we may think of Adam rejoicing with great joy at the thought, Mary, of your coming, as we know the Angels rejoiced, before the creation of the world, foreseeing your creation by God.

Chapter 8
Tuesday - Second Reading

Adam's punishment made him see the justice and mercy of God. Throughout his life he feared to offend God and was guided in all things by love for God. This way of life he handed on to those who came after him. With time they forgot God's justice and mercy. With time they forgot God himself, and that he was their Creator. They believed only what pleased them, immersing themselves in pleasure and sin.

So came the flood, when God destroyed all men on earth, saving only Noe and those with him in the Ark, through whom he willed to people the earth again. Once again men multiplied on the earth, and once again they fell, tempted away from God, turning to the worship of false gods and idols. God's mercy and fatherly love led him to intervene, and he chose one who was a faithful follower of his law, Abraham, to make a covenant with him and his descendants. He fulfilled his desire for a son, and Isaac was born. And he promised that from his descendants, Christ, his son, would come.

It is possible that Abraham, by God's permission, foresaw many things. We may think of him as having foreseen Mary, the Mother of Christ. We may think of him rejoicing in her, and loving her more than Isaac his son.

It was not greed or ambition that led Abraham to acquire lands and wealth. It was not for his own sake that he desired a son. He was like a gardener of some great lord's estate. He had planted a vine, and planned to make cuttings from that vine, and so in time make for his master a vineyard of great worth. Like a good gardener, he knew that each plant needed careful attention, and proper feeding, if it was to bear good fruit. One plant in particular he cherished, watching its growth with great delight. He knew that it would be the choicest of all the trees in his vineyard.

His master would love to rest in the shade beneath it, praising its beauty and the sweetness of its fruit. If Abraham was the gardener, then the vine which he first planted was Isaac; the cuttings of that vine his descendants; the feeding of each plant the goods of this world which Abraham acquired for the sake of Isaac and his race; the most cherished tree, that tree of beauty and sweetness, was the Virgin Mary; and the Master for whom Abraham the gardener worked, the owner of the vineyard, was God himself, who waited till the vineyard (the race of Isaac) was established, and then, coming, saw with content, the perfect vine in the midst of his vineyard, the Virgin Mother of God. The beauty of this tree was the perfect and sinless life of Mary; the sweetness of the fruit, the acts of her life; the shade of that tree, her virginal womb, overshadowed by the Spirit of God.

If Abraham then foresaw what was to be, he rejoiced in his many descendants, but most of all in that one of his descendants who, as Virgin Mother, was to bear the Son of God. This faith and holy desire Abraham handed on to Isaac, his son: your oath, he had said to the servant sent for Isaac's wife, must be sworn on the One who is to come of my race. Isaac too handed on this same faith and desire, when he blessed his son Jacob.

And Jacob in blessing his twelve sons, handed on this same faith and desire in his turn to Judah. God so loved Mary, the Mother of his Son, even before the creation of the world, and before her creating, that he gave to those he had specially chosen as his friends some foreknowledge of her, for their consolation. First to the Angels, then to Adam, and then to the Patriarchs, the creation of Mary was a thing of wonder and joy.

Chapter 9
Tuesday - Third Reading

God is all love, and all loving; infinite in love, and infinite in loving. We may truly say - God is love. He makes known his love to those who love, and all things speak to them of the love of God. See how great was his love for his People, the People of Israel. He delivered them from the Egyptians, and led them out from captivity, into a fruitful land, that they might live there in peace and prosperity. It was this prosperity that was envied by the Devil, and in his hatred for all that was loved by God, he tempted God's People, and by his deceits, led them time and and again into sin.

They had the Law of Moses; they were the People whom God had made his own, through his covenant with Abraham; yet they fell into idolatry and worshipped false gods. God looked on them and found there among them some who still served him with true faith and love, following his law. To strengthen these followers of his, amid the dangers that surrounded them, to confirm them in their faith and love, he raised up among them the Prophets, men who came not only for the help of God's own, but also to rescue those who had made themselves enemies of God.

In time, like the mountain streams which join, and then join to other streams as they descend, increasing ever in volume and power, carrying all before them, down at last to meet other waters and in the lower lands form into the great rivers, the Holy Ghost filled the hearts of his Prophets, and first one, then another, then more raised their voices, to speak as he inspired them, till their sound filled the ears of many, to comfort and console, to call back and restore. The sweetest sound of their voices was that news of joy - that God himself would be born of a Virgin, to make amends for the evil which Satan, through Adam, had caused to man; that he would redeem man, and rescue him from his misery, restoring to him eternal life.

Joy too, that God the Father so willed this redemption of man that he would not spare even his only-begotten Son: that the Son so willed to obey the Father, that he would take to himself our human flesh: that the Holy Ghost, though inseparable from the Father, willed to be sent by the Son. The Prophets knew that the Son of God would come into this world, to be light in our darkness, brighter than the sun at dawn, to proclaim God's justice and love. But they knew he would not come unheralded. As the morning star heralds the sun, they foresaw that a star would rise in Israel, fairest of all the stars, in brightness and beauty surpassed only by the sun itself. This star with the Virgin Mary, who would be Mother of Christ, her love surpassed only by the love of God, her heart ever responding to the will of God.

      This news was given by God to his Prophets, to console them in their labour of teaching, and encourage them in their trials.

      For they grieved at the pride and sinfulness of the People, who neglected the Law of Moses, rejected God's love, and incurred his anger. But they rejoiced, Mary, in you, foreseeing that God, that giver of all law, would receive back to his grace those who had sinned, for the sake of your humility and holiness of life. They grieved to see the Temple empty and desolate, and the worship of God neglected.

      They rejoiced, Mary, to foresee the creation of that holy temple, your pure body, where God himself would love to reside. They grieved at the destruction of the gates and the walls of the holy city, broken by armies, invaded by sin. They rejoiced, Mary, to foresee how you would stand firm, against all attack, a strong citadel where Christ would arm himself, the gate through which he would come forth to his conflict with the Devil and his own. To the Prophets, as to the Patriarchs, your coming, Mary, was a thing of wonder and joy.

Chapter 10
Wednesday - First Reading

Before God made known his law to Moses, man had to live without a rule of life. Those who loved God, did what they thought was God's will. Those who rejected his love, and did not fear to do so, acted as they chose. To dispel their ignorance, God in his goodness made known his law, teaching first the love of God, then love for others, then his will concerning marriage, its holiness and binding force, its purpose in his plan - the growth of his people. The union of man and woman in a holy marriage was most pleasing to God, for he willed to choose the child of such a union as the Mother of Christ. The eagle, flying above the earth, looks down at the trees, and choosing with its sharp eyes the tallest tree, one firmly rooted to withstand the storms, one that cannot be climbed, one that nothing can fall on, builds there its next, God sees, with penetrating gaze, all things, both present and future.

He looked therefore among all men and women, from the beginning to the end of time, for a husband and wife fit for the bearing of the child of his choice. He found none so worthy as Joachim and Anne, who lived together in holiness and a love for each other born of their love for him. It was to them he entrusted the one who was to be Mother of his Son. She was to be, as it were, the eagle's nest, in which he could find protection and shelter. Joachim and Anne were the tall tree in which this nest would be built, firmly rooted in a union based on the love and honour of God; the branches of this tree their lifelong thought for the will of God, and their desire for a child, not for their own sake, but to beget one who would grow to love God and serve him as they themselves did.

The tallness of this tree, beyond the reach of the winds, and higher than all around, was the height of holiness which Joachim and Anne had attained, beyond the attacks of Satan, untroubled, except by the thought that God's honour was many times assailed by the sins of many, with no thought of honour or worldly possessions, no pride or ambition to move them from their selfless love of God.

God knew that for the birth of the Mother of Christ, none holier could be found than Joachim and Anne. What a treasure you held, blessed Anne, while she who was to be Mother of God rested in your womb. How precious to God that seed of Mary's life in your womb, more precious than the offspring of all men on earth. Anne became God's treasure-house, keeping safe this most precious thing, this seed of so precious a life.

God saw it and watched over it, for as his Son was to say - where one's treasure is, there is one's heart. The Angels looked on this treasure with joy, knowing how precious it was to God their Creator. It was a holy and blessed day, to be honoured by all, the day when this precious seed was first sown. God himself and the Angels greeted that day with great rejoicing.

Chapter 11
Wednesday - Second Reading

That seed of life was ready, and at God's chosen moment, life began as he infused into it a living soul. We see the bees in summer, busy making flowers for honey; led by instinct to their sweetness, they seem often to wait for the buds to open. God foresaw, as he foresees all things, the birth of Mary, and he waited with joy as she lay hidden in her mother's womb, for he knew that none ever of those to be born would equal her in holiness. None would so make known to men his infinite love.

The infusing of Mary's soul in the womb of Blessed Anne was more beautiful than the dawn of the most beautiful day. As we so often long for the dawn, so Angels and men longed for her birth. Where the nights are short in summer, so that there is little darkness, people do not notice the dawn; they wait for the sun itself, thinking of their crops and their fruits. Where the nights are quite long, even in summer, the dawn is watched for and welcomed, not only for the coming of the sun to the fields, but because men weary of the night and the darkness.

The Angels in heaven did not await the coming of Mary that they might see Christ, for they were ever in the light of his presence; they longed for her, so that the love of God might be made known in the world, so that men who loved God might be strengthened in their love, and then they, the Angels, could go out to gather them as an everlasting harvest for God. But men, living in this world of sorrow and hardship, desired the coming of Mary that they might see Christ their Saviour. They longed for her coming, that they might learn from her perfect life how man should live. The Virgin Mary is foretold as the branch which would grow from the root of the father of David, to bear a flower on which the Spirit of God would rest. In her mother's womb - how light Anne's burden! - Mary was the tender branch which would soon come forth. The flower that branch would bear was Christ.

He himself, from the moment of her assent to God's message, was a richer and infinitely sweeter nourishment than blessed Anne had given to her. Though Mary was to him the food of life, giving her own flesh and blood to be his, that he might appear in true humanity, he was to Mary her heavenly food, that she might bear him as her child, though he was truly the Son of God. They were Mother and Son, Son and Mother, yet this Son was truly the Son of God, the only-begotten Son of the Father, eternally with him, eternally united with him and the Holy Ghost, eternally the Person of the Son of God, who with the Father and the Spirit lives in glory, eternally One.

Chapter 12
Wednesday - Third Reading

In Father, Son and Holy Ghost, there is only the one Divinity. There is ever the one divine will. A fire with three flames is but the one fire. The three flames of love in God are the one love of his will, burning to fulfil his one divine purpose. The love of the Father was seen most brightly by the Angels when they knew his will to give his Son for the redemption of man. The love of the Son proceeding from the Father was seen most brightly when the son willed to deprive himself of his glory and take the form of a slave.

The love of the Holy Ghost was seen most brightly in that readiness to make known in many ways the one will of the Three. All heaven was ablaze with these flames of God's love, to the delight of the Angels. Yet all heaven must wait; must wait for the coming of Mary. The redemption of man, willed and foreseen by God, could not take place without her. A flame of divine love was to be kindled in Mary which would rise up to God and return so filled with his love that no corner of this world would be left cold and in darkness.

When Mary was born, she was like a new lamp, all ready to be lit; to be lit by God with a light burning like the three-fold flame of his own love. The first flame of her lover was her choice, for God's glory, to be ever a virgin. So pleasing was this to the Father that he willed to entrust to her his beloved Son, that Son who is inseparable from the Divinity of himself and the Holy Ghost. The second flame of her love was her humility, so pleasing to the Son that he willed to take from her a true human body, and that humanity which was destined to be honoured in heaven above all things. The third flame of her love was her obedience, which brought to her from the Holy Ghost the fullness of grace.

It is true that these flames of Mary's love were not lit at the moment of her birth. She was still, as other children, only a little one, unaware of God's will. Yet God took more pleasure in her than in all other beings. She was like a sweet-sounding harp, not yet in tune; but he whose treasure she was knew how lovely the music he would make with her.

It may be believed that Christ's knowledge was not lacking in anything due when he was conceived in Mary's womb. We may believe too that Mary developed in understanding earlier than others. Since the coming of Mary was such joy to God and the Angels, men too must rejoice, and give glory and honour to God, who chose her from all his creation by eternal decree and willed that she should be born among sinners, to bring forth in sinlessness the Saviour of the world.

Chapter 13
Thursday - First Reading

Speaking of the beauty of Mary, we think of lovely things: her sacred body is like a vase of purest crystal; her soul like a lantern of clearest light; her mind like a fountain of water rising up into the air, then falling in cool streams to the deep valley. Passing from infancy to childhood, to the age when she was able to understand, she began to think of the existence of God, and how he made all things, and especially man, for his own eternal glory, and how his justice embraces all things.

Her thoughts reached out to God, as the waters of the fountain rise into the air; then, like those waters flowing down to the valley, her thoughts returned to herself and brought her a most profound humility. The Church sings of Christ leaving and returning to the Father, though he was ever with the Father and the Father ever with him. Mary's thoughts reached up to heaven in contemplation and grasped God by faith. Then in the love with which God possessed her, she turned her mind again to God and to herself, never losing her thought of God. Together with hope and trust, and with holy fear, the fire of this love inflamed her heart, as the flame is the brightness of the lantern.

She understood the perfect subjection of body to soul, and no discord ever troubled her, so that in body she was purer than purest crystal. How soon she learnt to appreciate God's love, and treasure it with all her being! Think of this love as a lily which God had planted, with a threefold root, bearing three flowers of great beauty. The three roots are three most powerful virtues, protecting her body. The three flowers, three adornments of her soul, which gave great joy to God and the Angels.

The first of the three virtues was her abstinence, her right use of God's gifts of food and drink - no over-indulgence to make her slow in the service of God, no unwise austerity to impair her health. The second was her wakefulness, so that she rested no longer than was necessary - not wasting God's time in laziness, but not fatiguing herself to the detriment of her work. The third was her command over her will, so that she was not easily wearied in body, and never over-anxious or over-excited.

The first adornment of her soul was her love for the things of God rather than the things of earth, no matter how beautiful these might seem to be. The things men so often prize, possessions and wealth, were utterly distasteful to her. The second adornment was her appreciation of the infinite distance between worldly honours and spiritual glory. This world's praises were as abhorrent to her as the poisoning air of corruption. The third adornment was her love for all that God loves, her repugnance for all that was hateful and displeasing to him. She sought in all things the true sweetness of God, and no taste of bitterness was permitted to endure in her after her death.

With such beauty of soul, Mary surpassed all other created things. God willed that only through her should his promise be fulfilled. Her love left no blemish or defect, not even the smallest. In nothing could the enemy claim victory over her. If then she was so pleasing in the sight of God and the Angels, may we not think that she had also great earthly beauty? Those who saw her looked with delight, and knew that her loveliness was born of her love for God. They saw her, and loved to see her, and were led to a new love for God.

They watched her, and loved to be with her, and knew that no evil could touch them, nothing sinful attract them, in the presence of her beauty and holiness.

Chapter 14
Thursday - Second Reading

With our slow and clouded minds, it is hard for us to appreciate that moment when Mary first knew God and gave herself to him. His will became her one desire and her joy. She saw how she owed everything to his creating; but she knew that according to his plan, her will was free, to choose or refuse his will and his way. She saw the blessings which God had already bestowed, and for these alone she chose to love him in return, and to love him for ever.

Soon she was to understand how much more he would do, She learnt that he who created all would not rest content, but would himself come to his creation as redeemer of his creatures. And this out of love alone. She learnt that man's will, free to choose good or evil, could make satisfaction to God for sin, or incur his anger by sin. In that moment of understanding, she chose once for all her course through life.

The captain of a ship knows what dangers lie ahead, and he charts his voyage to avoid the storms. He watches the ship's course, and works out the distance sailed, and the distance still to sail before arriving in port. Every rope, every piece of equipment is in place and ready for use. The cargo he carries must reach port as quickly as possible. Every detail of the voyage must be worked out ahead. Mary was like the captain of a ship.

As soon as she had understood God's will, she set her course according to his commandments. She was watchful at all times that her attention should never be distracted from God. She took care, when those around her spoke of their ambitions, their successes or failures, not to let herself become less devout in her service of God. Anything contrary to God's law she knew at once as a danger to be avoided at all cost.

With this self-training and discipline, all that she did was good. All that she said, all that she listened to, all that she gave her attention to, was sensible and wise.

Her work was useful to herself and to others, and each journey she made had some good reason. The trials of life she accepted with patience and joy. Her one thought was God. Her one desire was to be for ever with him, to offer to him in return for all he had done for her all her love and her praise. So perfect a life won her from God, who is the giver of all good things, the highest holiness and glory. It is no wonder that God lover her more than all other creatures.

She alone of all men and women was ever sinless and immune from sin. How near she was to heaven at that moment when the Angel Gabriel greeted her - Hail, full of grace! How pure, how holy she was, at that moment when the Father entrusted to her his only Son, at her assenting - Be it done unto me, according to thy word! At that moment of time, Divinity was united with humanity, humanity with Divinity; the Son of God was made man; the Son of the Father become the Son of Mary.

Chapter 15
Thursday - Third Reading

This union between God and man, between Christ and the Virgin Mary, only God can comprehend. The Son of God, truly God, all present and present to all, whose eternal dwelling in heaven is the Blessed Trinity itself, made for himself on earth a dwelling-place in the womb of the Virgin Mary. The Holy Ghost, who is ever in the Father and in the Son, rested in Mary, filling her, both body and soul, with his presence. The Son, who is ever with the Father and the Holy Ghost in heaven, acquired for himself as man a new dwelling on earth. The Father too, with the Holy Ghost, dwelt in a new way on earth, in the humanity of the Son, for the Father with the Holy Ghost must be ever in the Son. The Son alone took flesh.

He alone took our humanity. True God, he came as man to men, withholding from the eyes of men his Divinity seen ever by the Angels in heaven. All who hold the true faith must rejoice unceasingly at this union achieved through Mary. The Son of God took in her womb true flesh and blood, and true humanity, not losing his Divinity: in divinity was humanity, in humanity Divinity. Christ did not lose his Divinity, nor Mary her virginity.

It would be utterly wrong to think that God could not have done such a thing, for all things are possible to God. It would be equally wrong to think that he would not have done such a thing for his own, for this would deny the goodness of God. If we believe then that God could and would do such a thing, why do not all men love God with all their love?

Picture some king, honoured by all, with great power and possessions, and someone dear to him suffering great insult and injury; if the king took on himself the burden of his friend, if he gave all his wealth to save him from poverty, still more, if he offered his life for his friend, would not this be the greatest love he could show? But no love of men on earth could equal the love of God in heaven. No love could equal that love which led God to condescend to our need, and entrust himself to the womb of the Virgin Mary and take there our humanity.

Mary is like that bush which Moses saw, burning yet never consumed by the fire. God himself was there, till Moses knew and obeyed his word. And to him he made known his name - I am who am, the name of the eternal. The Son of God dwelt in Mary, till the span of time between conception and birth was completed. At conception, he had taken, by his Divinity, full possession of Mary's pure body. At birth he came forth, with his Divinity united for ever to true humanity. But as the sweet perfume of the rose leaves the rose still as lovely, his coming forth was no lessening, but truly a glorification of the virginity of Mary.

To God, to the Angels, to Adam, to the Patriarchs and the Prophets, and to countless servants of God, this Burning Bush, which was Mary, brought joy beyond words - Mary, in the fire of her love, conceiving the Son of God - the Son of God in obedience to the Father, resting in her, to be born, true man, true God, of a Mother and Virgin, a Virgin-Mother. To ourselves also, and to all our race, this must bring great rejoicing and consolation. The Son of God, he who with the Father and the Spirit is the eternal God, has taken our humanity, through the love of the Virgin Mary.

Her love embraces all things that belong to God. We then may claim, and be sure of her intercession. We can say truly than man who deserved eternal death through sin can acquire eternal life only through her. From Mary, the Son of God came in perfect humanity, to fight as man with Satan who had subjugated man. To Mary, men must resort for strength against Satan's temptings. Mary is the gateway by which Christ entered into this world, to open to man the gate of heaven. Pray then, pray then to Mary, that at death she may come to us, to secure for us entry into the eternal kingdom of Christ, her Son.

Chapter 16
Friday - First Reading

We are told that Mary was afraid when the Angel appeared and spoke to her. It was not fear of any bodily harm to herself, but dismay at the thought that this might be a trick of Satan, to lead her into sin. At the moment when her mind first knew God and his holy will, she had chosen for herself a life of love, and this brought with it a wise and holy fear of God.

It is our delight to call Mary a rose of great beauty. We know that the lovelier and healthier the rose, the stronger and sharper are the thorns which surround it. It Mary is a rose of beauty, she will not be untouched by the sharp thorns or trial and sorrow. Indeed, as the days of her life went by, her sorrows increased in bitterness and pressed more heavily upon her. Her first sorrow was that fear of God which her knowledge of his existence and his will had brought her. It was a sorrow to her that in all she did, she must keep in mind the thought and threat of sin. She directed each thought, word and work to God, but there was always the fear that some defect might creep in to lessen its value in his eyes. How foolish are those who deliberately and without fear throw themselves into all kinds of sin, bringing on themselves suffering and sorrow.

Mary was sinless, and immune from sin. Everything she did pleased God. In every way she was entirely pleasing to him. Yet she never allowed herself to be free from the fear of displeasing him. A greater sorrow still was in her heart, for she knew from the writings of the Prophets that God willed to come as man, and suffer as man. In her love for God, this caused her great grief, though she did not yet know that she was to be the Mother of God. When that moment arrived, the moment when she knew that the Son of God had become her Son, to take in her womb that human body which was to suffer as the Prophets had foretold - who could measure her joy?

Who could measure her sorrow? Like the rose, she had grown in beauty, but the thorns had grown too, stronger and sharper and more piercing. To Mary it was joy beyond words that her son should come in humility to lead man to heaven, saving him from the penalty which Adam's pride had incurred, the misery of hell. It was great sorrow that the sin of Adam by which man rebelled in both body and soul should require the redeeming death of her Son in such agony of body and soul.

It was great joy to her to conceive her Son in sinlessness and purity. It was great sorrow to her that this so loved son was born to suffer a shameful death, and that she herself would be there to stand and see. Great joy to know that he would rise from death, and win in return for his Passion an everlasting honour and glory; great sorrow to know that this glory would not be won except by the agony and shame of the Cross. The perfect rose blooms in beauty on its stem, and our delight is not spoiled by the sharp thorns around it.

The sharp thorns of Mary's sorrow piercing her heart could not change her or weaken her will, and in her suffering she accepted whatever God's will should demand of her. We call her a Rose of Jericho, for men say that nowhere can so lovely a rose be found. In her holiness, Mary is more beautiful than all mankind, surpassed only by her Son. To God and the Angels in heaven, her patience and willing endurance brought joy. To all on earth, it must be a joy to meditate on her sufferings so willingly accepted, and on that consolation she had ever in her heart, that all was the will of God.

Chapter 17
Friday - Second Reading

The Prophets foretold many things about Christ. They spoke of the death of the Innocent One and the pains he would suffer to win for men on earth an eternal life with him in heaven. They foretold and set in writing that the Son of God, to save all men, would be bound, scourged, mocked, led out to be crucified, and reviled as he hung on the Cross. They knew that the immortal God would take man's mortal form. They knew that he willed to suffer as man for man.

If the Prophets foresaw these things, would not Mary foresee them, even more clearly? She was the Mother predestined for the Son of God. How could she not have foreseen his sufferings when he took flesh in her womb for this very purpose? The presence of the Holy Ghost would enlighten her, so that she knew better than the Prophets that things which they, through the Holy Ghost, foretold.

At the moment of Christ's birth, as she held him for the first time in her arms, Mary foresaw the fulfilment of prophecy. As she wrapped him in swaddling-clothes, she foresaw the scourging of his flesh which would make him a leper in the eyes of men. The hands and feet of her Child brought the thought of the nails which would pierce them. The face of her Son, beautiful beyond the beauty of men, was the face men would spit on. His cheeks would feel the blows of their hatred. His ears would hear the curses of their defiance.

His eyes would be blinded by the blood from the wounds in his head. His mouth would taste the bitterness of gall. His arms would be bound, then stretched in agony on the Cross; and his heart, empty at last of blood, would shrink in death. No part of that sacred body would escape the bitterness of that most bitter death. And when all breathing ceased, there would still be the soldier's sharp spear to pierce his lifeless heart. Mary rejoiced as no mother ever rejoiced when her Son, the Son of God, was born, true God, true man, mortal in his humanity, immortal in his Divinity.

But Mary knew sorrow deeper than the sorrows of all mothers, foreseeing the Passion of her Son. Her joy was beyond words, but her joy brought with it a sorrow deeper than all the sorrows of this world.

A mother's joy is complete when her child is born and she sees it healthy and perfectly formed. Her pain and anxiety are over. Mary rejoiced at Christ's birth, but she knew that no moment of her life would be free of sorrow. The Prophets foretold, long before the coming of Christ, his sufferings and death. Simeon foretold, in the presence of Mary and her Child, the piercing of her heart by a sword of sorrow. We know that the mind is more sensitive to pain even than the body.

We know that the soul of Mary, even before the death of her Son, would feel that sword of sorrow more sharply than all women on earth would feel the suffering of childbearing. Each day brought nearer the sufferings of Christ. Each day brought nearer the piercing of Mary's heart. It was the compassion of Christ alone which enabled her, by his presence and his words, to bear day by day such piercing sorrow.

Chapter 18
Friday - Third Reading

You shall seek me and shall not find me'. These words of Christ were the sharp point of the sword of sorrow, entering Mary's heart. That sword pierced deeper at the betrayal of Judas, and at the arrest of Christ, when he willed to be taken by the enemies of justice and truth. Deeper still at each insult offered to Christ, with each suffering inflicted on him. The sorrow of her heart overflowed into all the members of her body. She saw how cruelly Christ was struck, and more cruelly beaten and scourged. She heard the sentence of death passed by the Jews. She heard the cries of the people - Crucify him, away with him.

She saw him led out, bound as a criminal, to a traitor's death. She saw him struggling to carry his Cross, dragged forward and whipped as he stumbled, led like some wild beast rather than a lamb to the slaughter. As Isaias had foretold, he went meekly to his death; like the lamb that is led to the slaughter house, like the sheep that is dumb before its shearers.

Christ was patient in his sufferings. Mary endured patiently the sorrow of his sufferings. She followed him, even to the place of death. She saw the wounds of his scourging, the crown of thorns, his cheeks disfigured with blows, his face covered with blood, and she wept in sorrow.

She saw him stretched on the Cross, and heard the blows of the hammer as the nails pierced his hands and feet. So great was her suffering and sorrow that her strength almost failed her as she stood by and watched. She saw the vinegar and gall offered for his lips to taste. and her own lips could not move in prayer. She heard his cry - My God, My God, why hast thou forsaken me?, and saw his head fall forward and his body become rigid as he breathed forth his spirit. She stood and saw how he died. Then truly was her heart quite pierced by the sword of sorrow. It was the strength God gave that alone saved her from dying in such sorrow. To see her Son, stripped and bleeding, dying, pierced by a lance, mocked by those who stood by, jeered at by soldiers, deserted by all but a few of his chosen ones, abandoned by so many whom he had won to justice and truth, to see this most bitter death - could there be sorrow so deep as her?

We read that once, when the Ark of God fell into the hands of enemies, the wife of one of God's priests died for sorrow. How much greater was the sorrow of Mary, for she saw the body of her Son, which the Ark prefigured, nailed to the wood of the Cross. Her love for her Son was love for the Son of God, greater than the loves of all men. If the loss of the Ark could cause sorrow and death, the death of Christ would have brought Mary to death but for God's gift to support so grievous a sorrow. By his death, Christ opened the gateway to heaven, and won for his own their entry into joy. Mary looked up from the depths of her sorrow, as one coming back from the gates of death.

Her faith never faltered that Christ would rise again, and in this faith she could comfort many whose faith had failed. They took him down from the Cross, and wrapped him in fine linen with spices, and laid him in the tomb. Then all left. Few still had faith that he would rise. Little by little, the sorrows of Mary's heart lightened, and she felt the first sweetness of consolation. The sufferings of her Son were at an end. She knew that on the third day he would rise, would rise with his humanity united again to his Divinity, would rise to everlasting honour and glory, to suffer, to die no more.

Chapter 19
Saturday - First Reading

We read that the Queen of Sheba made the long journey from her own lands in the south to visit Solomon the King. Her journey was not wasted, for she found great delight in his words. No gifts were too precious for her to give, no praise too high, and she departed in admiration of such great wisdom. The Virgin Mary spent long hours in thought, considering the course of events in this world, and all the things that this world holds dear. Nothing delighted or attracted her, except the wisdom she had learned from God. This was her desire and her search, and she did not rest till she had found it in Christ.

In the Son of God she found wisdom infinitely greater than Solomon's. The Queen of Sheba was overcome with wonder as she contemplated the wisdom of Solomon. Mary was overcome with sorrow as she pondered the loving wisdom of Christ, who saw salvation in suffering, and willed to save man from subjection to Satan by his sufferings and cross. When at last the sufferings of Christ were over, Mary looked up from the depths of her sorrow, ever offering herself and her will to God for his glory, gifts most precious to him. Gifts too of another kind, for many were led to the truth of God by her faith.

No words or works of men were so powerful to bring men to God. Many lost faith when they saw Christ die. She alone withstood the unbelief of men, seeing in Christ her Son the Son of God, over whose Godhead death could have no dominion.

When the third day came, it brought bewilderment and anxiety to the Disciples. The women going to the tomb to anoint the body of Jesus sought him and could not find him. The Apostles were gathered together in their fear, guarding the doors. Then, surely, though we are not told of this in the Gospels, Mary spoke of the resurrection of her Son, that he had truly risen from death, that he was alive again in all his humanity, no more subject to death, risen to an eternal glory. We read that Mary Magdalen and the Apostles were first to see the risen Christ. But we may believe that Mary his Mother knew of his rising before all others, and that she was the first to see him.

It was Mary in her lowliness who first gave praise and adoration to the risen Christ. When Christ ascended to the glory of his kingdom, the Virgin Mary remained on earth. We cannot know what her presence meant to so many. Those who loved God were strengthened in their love; those who had turned from him were brought back to his love. The Apostles looked to her for guidance and counsel. The Martyrs found in her, courage to face suffering and death. The Confessors of the Faith were strengthened in their believing. Virgins were drawn to her purity. Widows were consoled by her sorrows. Husbands and wives found in her a pattern of perfection. All who heard and obeyed the word of God found in Mary great comfort and help.

Whenever the Apostles came to her, she was able to teach them about Christ, and help them to understand. The Martyrs rejoiced to suffer for Christ, for he had suffered for all. They remembered the long years of sorrow borne so patiently by Mary his Mother, and they bore their martyrdom even more readily. The Confessors, meditating on Mary, learnt many things about the truths of the Faith. From her example, they learnt too the wise use of earthly things, food, drink and sleep, work and rest.

And how to order their lives in all things to the honour and glory of God. Virgins learnt from Mary's example true chastity in virtue. They learnt too the wise use of their time, how to avoid vanity and foolish talk, and see all things in the light of true holiness. Widows learnt from her, consolation in sorrow, strength against temptation, and humble submission to God's will. With a mother's love, Mary could never have wished for the death of her Son, still less for the death of the Son of God. Yet she willed in all things the will of God. She chose for God's sake the humble acceptance of suffering and sorrow.

Husbands and wives learnt from Mary true love for each other, in body and in soul, and the union of their wills, as of their flesh, in all that the will of God demanded. They learnt how she had united herself for ever with God by faith, and never in any way shown resistance to his divine will.

Chapter 20
Saturday - Second Reading

We read in the Gospels these words of Christ - the measure you give shall be the measure you receive. No one on earth can know the glory of Mary, the Mother of God. She who on earth gave so much receives now in heaven a measure of glory beyond the whole of creation. When it pleased Christ to call her from this earth, there awaited her all whom her holiness had helped. God himself, whose love had been made known only through her, awaited her coming to adorn her with a glory surpassed only by his own. She was raised to the highest place in heaven, to be Queen, not only of his earthly creation, but Queen over the Angels for ever.

The Angels rejoiced in this Queen, made for ever obedient to her by their love for her. Those Angels too who had fallen from God were made subject to her; not temptation of theirs could withstand her; no one calling with love for her help would be left unprotected; the tempters would choose rather an increase of their misery than the opposing of her power. Of all creatures the most humble, Mary is now the most glorious, the most perfect in beauty, and nearest to God himself. As gold surpassed all other metals, Angels and men surpass all the creatures of God. Gold needs the fire and the work of the goldsmith before it can be fashioned into a work of beauty.

Mary, more perfect than all Angels and men, was fashioned by her own will, in the fire of the Holy Ghost, into a thing of the highest beauty. A work of art wrought in gold needs the light to be seen; in the light of the sun, it will be seen in all its perfection. All that the Virgin Mary accomplished, and the beauty of her soul, could not be seen while she was living on earth. Lit by the light of God himself in heaven, she appeared in the fulness of beauty. All heaven gave praise to her, and to that beauty of soul with which her will had adorned her, a beauty beyond the beauty of all creation, near even to God's own perfection. Mary is enthroned for ever, on that throne placed near to the throne of God.

No one is nearer than she to the Father, the Son and the Holy Ghost. The Father is in the Son, the Son is in the Father, the Holy Ghost is in the Father and the Son. The Son, when he became man in the Virgin's womb, was not thereby divided from the Father and the Holy Ghost. He took our humanity, not losing his Divinity, as Mary acquired Motherhood without loss to her Virginity. God gave to Mary, therefore, a place near to himself, so that she is ever with the Father, the Son and the Holy Ghost, and ever associated with this Blessed Trinity in all things.

Who could measure the joy in heaven when God raised Mary from this earth? Who will measure our joy when, seeing God face to face, we see too the glory of Mary? The Angels rejoicing in Mary glorify God. The death of Christ has filled again the places made vacant in heaven. The raising of Mary to heaven has increased even the blessedness of heaven. To Adam and Eve, to the Patriarchs and Prophets, to all who died before Christ and were released by his death, to all who have died since Christ's death and been taken to heaven, Mary's entry into heaven is an everlasting joy and delight.

They praise God for her glory, for the honour he has bestowed on her as the one who bore in holiness Christ, their Redeemer and Lord. We may picture the Apostles and many holy ones around Mary as her last hour approached. We know the reverence and honour they paid to her at the moment of her death. We believe that she died, as all others die. We believe that her Son, the Son of God, took her to himself, and raised her, body and soul, to live for ever in heaven.

Chapter 21
Saturday - Third Reading

The Son of God, the Son of Mary, Christ who is Truth itself, has said to us - return not evil for evil, but return good for evil. Will not he himself therefore, for he is God, return good for good, and five great reward even for little? He promises in the Gospel that for every good work he will repay a hundredfold. What then will be Mary's reward? Her life was a life of countless good works, a life entirely pleasing to God, a life ever free from defect and unmarred by sin. In all things her will chose, and every member of her body responded gladly to that command. The justice of God has willed that we must rise, body and soul, at the last day, to be repaid for our works.

Body and soul we shall stand before God, for in all things, body and soul act as one. Christ's sinless body rose from the dead, and is now and for ever united in glory with his Divinity. The sinless body of Mary, together with her soul, was taken up by God after her death into heaven, and she is honoured there, body and soul, for ever. No mind of ours can comprehend the perfection and glory which is Christ's as reward for his sufferings. No mind of ours can comprehend the glory which is Mary's, in body and soul, for her perfect obedience to God.

The holiness of Mary, those virtues adorning her soul, glorified God her Creator, and she is crowned now in heaven with his reward for those virtues.

The good works of Mary, accomplished by her perfect subjection of body to soul, proclaim for ever her praise. She has done all things as God willed, and omitted nothing that God desired, to win an eternal heavenly glory of both body and soul. No soul, except Christ's, was so filled with holiness and merit as the pure soul of Mary. No body, except the sacred body of her Son, was so worthy to be glorified for its purity and perfection as the pure body of Mary. The justice of God flashed forth when he drove Adam from the garden of Paradise for tasting the forbidden fruit of the tree of knowledge. The mercy of God entered sweetly into this world when the Virgin Mary was born, whom we may fittingly name the tree of life.

The justice of God drove out Adam and Eve into instant exile and misery, for their disobeying. The mercy of God gently invites and attracts to the glory of heaven, all who seek life in obeying. Mary, the tree of life, grew up in this world, to the joy of the Angels in heaven. They longed for the fruit of this tree, which was Christ, and they rejoiced, as they rejoiced in their own eternal happiness, that the great love of God would be made known among men, and their own heavenly ranks increased in number.

The Angel Gabriel rejoiced to be sent with God's message to Mary, and his greeting was spoken with great love for her. When Mary, in the perfection of her holiness and humility, assented, he rejoiced still more that the desire of all the Angels was soon to be fulfilled. We believe and we know, that Mary was assumed body and soul into heaven. We and all our race should ever think of her, and pray to her. In the trials and sorrows of our days, in the sinfulness of our hearts, in the bitterness of life, overshadowed by the certain approach of death. we should look to her, and draw near to her with true sorrow for sin.

We have called her the tree of life. To taste the fruit of the tree, we must first part its branches, and stretch out our hands through the leaves. The tree of life is Mary, the sweet fruit of this tree, Christ her Son. We reach through the branches to pluck the fruit when we greet Mary, as Gabriel did, with great love. She offers us her sweet fruit to taste when she sees our hearts no longer in sin, but willing in all things the will of God. Her intercession and prayer help us to receive the most holy Body of Christ, consecrated for us by the hands of men. This is the Food of true Life, the bread of Angels, and the nourishment of sinful men.

We, though we are sinful and sinning - we are the desire of Christ. His own blood has redeemed us, and he has destined us for heaven, to increase there the numbers of his loved ones. With wise thought, therefore, and with care, with all reverence and love, take him and eat. Let Christ fulfil in you this desire of his heart.

May the wondrous intercession of the Virgin whose name is Mary win for you this joy from her Son, Jesus Christ, who, with the Father and the Holy Ghost, lives and reigns, God for ever. Amen.

Printed in Great Britain
by Amazon